Athletic Trainers

Careers in Healthcare

Athletic Trainers

Jennifer Hunsaker

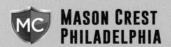

MASON CREST
PHILADELPHIA

Mason Crest
450 Parkway Drive, Suite D
Broomall, PA 19008
www.masoncrest.com

Printed and bound in the United States of America.

CPSIA Compliance Information: Batch #CHC2017.
For further information, contact Mason Crest at 1-866-MCP-Book.

First printing
1 3 5 7 9 8 6 4 2

Library of Congress Cataloging-in-Publication Data

on file at the Library of Congress
ISBN: 978-1-4222-3795-3 (hc)
ISBN: 978-1-4222-7983-0 (ebook)

Careers in Healthcare series ISBN: 978-1-4222-3794-6

QR CODES AND LINKS TO THIRD-PARTY CONTENT

Table of Contents

KEY ICONS TO LOOK FOR:

Words to understand: These words with their easy-to-understand definitions will increase the reader's understanding of the text while building vocabulary skills.

Sidebars: This boxed material within the main text allows readers to build knowledge, gain insights, explore possibilities, and broaden their perspectives by weaving together additional information to provide realistic and holistic perspectives.

Educational Videos: Readers can view videos by scanning our QR codes, providing them with additional educational content to supplement the text. Examples include news coverage, moments in history, speeches, iconic sports moments and much more!

Text-dependent questions: These questions send the reader back to the text for more careful attention to the evidence presented there.

Research projects: Readers are pointed toward areas of further inquiry connected to each chapter. Suggestions are provided for projects that encourage deeper research and analysis.

Series glossary of key terms: This back-of-the book glossary contains terminology used throughout this series. Words found here increase the reader's ability to read and comprehend higher-level books and articles in this field.

According to the National Athletic Trainer's Association (NATA) an athletic trainer is a highly trained health care professional that works with physicians to provide emergency care, preventative services, and rehabilitation of injuries and medical conditions.

 # Words to Understand in This Chapter

acute—referring to an injury or illness that requires immediate attention.

allied health care profession—a medical field in which trained people work with physicians, nurses, dentists, and pharmacists to provide patient care in exercise, health education, and daily functioning.

chronic—referring to an injury or illness that lasts a long time or constantly recurs.

kinesiology—The study of muscular movement, especially the mechanics of human motion.

risk factors—anything that makes a person more likely to become ill or injured; for example, being overweight, having high blood pressure, living in a toxic environment, or using poor form while exercising.

treatment plan—for a person who is sick or injured, a list of goals and ways of achieving them so the person can regain health and well-being.

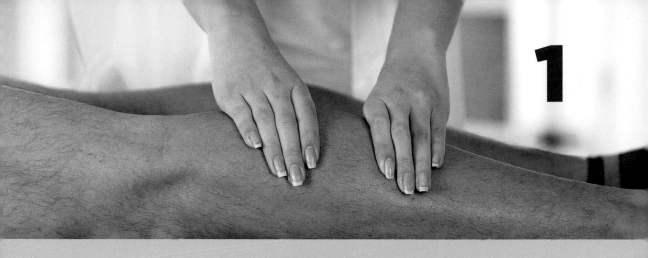

1

What Does an Athletic Trainer Do?

Sitting at a football game on a fall afternoon, you see a player lying down in the field after a big play. Two people run onto the field and kneel next to the injured player, asking questions, testing his ability to move, and ultimately helping him to the sidelines for further evaluation. These are athletic trainers in action. But an AT's responsibility extends far beyond the field of play.

The Roles of the Athletic Trainer

Athletic trainers work under the direction of a doctor to help prevent, diagnose, and treat injuries that occur as a result of movement. This means that everyone who moves—not just athletes—can benefit from the expertise of an athletic trainer. Recognized by the American Medical Association (AMA) as

In addition to working on muscle and bone injuries, athletic trainers are trained to assess athletes for concussions.

an *allied health care profession*, athletic training is starting to play a role in hospitals and clinics as well as jobs that require physical endurance.

All tasks athletic trainers perform fall into one of five areas: (1) injury prevention, (2) evaluation and diagnosis, (3) emergency care, (4) treatment and rehabilitation, and (5) professional health and well-being.

Injury Prevention

An athletic trainer's first goal is to help people stay injury-free. From minor sprains to major head injuries, ATs assess their patients for *risk factors* that could mean a patient has a greater chance of becoming ill or injured during physical activity. They do this by performing physical exams before a patient begins exercising or playing sports, checking for flexibility and muscle endurance, examining a person's posture and body composition, and assessing heart health. Once ATs identify any potential problems, they recommend ways to help a person strengthen her body, eat right, stay hydrated, and keep her body healthy and injury-free.

An AT's interest in injury prevention is not limited to athletics. An increasing number of manufacturing, construction, and industrial businesses are using the expertise of athletic trainers to make their workplaces safer. An AT's efforts may be as personal as working with an employee to improve his lifting posture or as far-reaching as requiring secondary safety harnesses to keep workers upright. Using their knowledge of

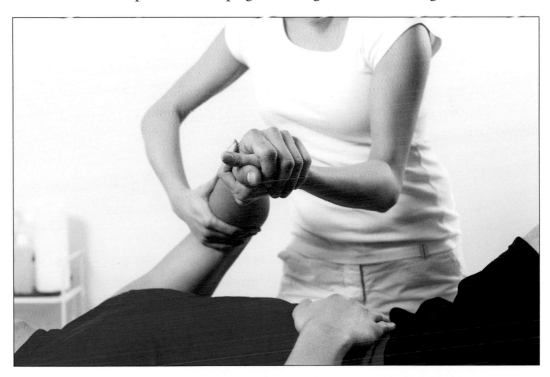

While often confused with personal trainers, athletic trainers are allied health care professionals.

The First Time I "Felt" Like a Trainer

When asked what real-life experience has affected her practice as an athletic trainer, one woman told the following story:

"During a clinical rotation, one of the track and field athletes at the university came in complaining of back pain. My preceptor (the supervising professor) had worked with her on a few injuries before and dismissed it as nothing. My gut told me differently, but I didn't want to go against what this particular preceptor was advising. A few days passed and the athlete came back complaining of the same back pain, which the preceptor dismissed once again.

"I took her aside, performed a few diagnostic tests, and told her what I believed it to be, then recommended that she see one of the team physicians about it. She did, and it turned out I was right! She came back to me a few days later, gave me a hug, and thanked me for helping her.

"That was when I realized I was in the right place."

anatomy and *kinesiology*, ATs can spot potential problems in a business and offer managers guidelines for addressing those problems.

Evaluation and Diagnosis

Athletic trainers are trained to evaluate and diagnose *acute* or *chronic* injuries to a person's muscles and bones. To do this,

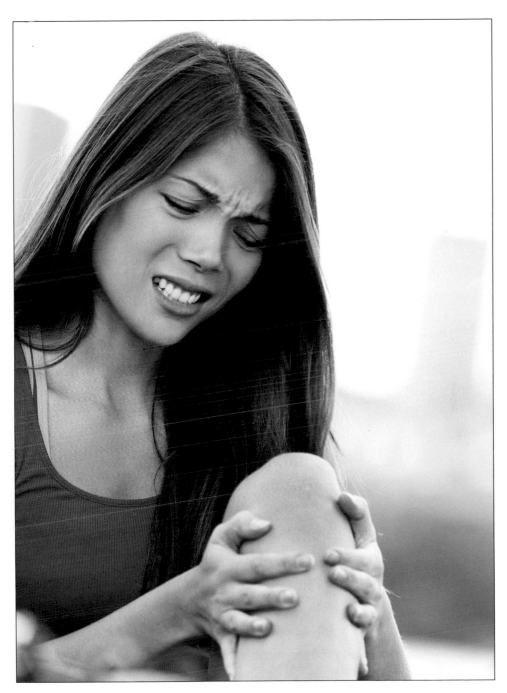

Athletic injuries can happen at any time, not just during a game or match.

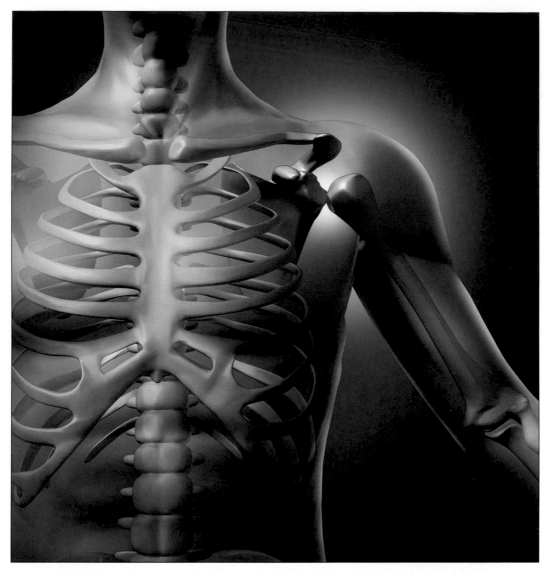

Athletic trainers are able to use a variety of diagnostic techniques to assess injuries.

ATs must have a thorough understanding of how the body works as well as how the body becomes injured. When a patient is injured, ATs watch the person move, feel the injured body part with their hands, and perform special tests to see how the bone and muscle work (or don't work). They can then diagnose the person's injury and begin to create a *treatment plan* to help him get better. In some cases, ATs may refer a patient to another health care professional for an x-ray, an ultrasound, an MRI, or a CT scan to determine the severity of the injury.

Emergency Care

Sometimes a person may become severely injured while under the watchful eye of an athletic trainer. ATs are the first responders in these situations, assessing and treating injuries until other medical professionals can transport the injured person to a hospital. In life-threatening situations, ATs can perform cardiopulmonary resuscitation (CPR), use drugs and a defibrillator to help get a person's heart to start beating again, control bleeding, put a splint on a broken bone, or use a spine board to help prevent further injury to a patient. In non–life-threatening emergencies, ATs are trained to manage head injuries, seizures, diabetes, asthma, shock, allergic reactions, and a host of other emergencies until the injured or ill person can be treated by a physician.

Treatment and Rehabilitation

Once people become injured, ill, or disabled, or if they have undergone surgery, athletic trainers use their knowledge of the body to create a treatment plan to help them regain their health and mobility. Treatment plans are always tailored to the person and the injury. They may include exercises to improve balance,

Educational Video

For an overview of an athletic trainer's job, scan here:

strength, and flexibility. They may also call for electrical stimulation, massage, or braces and splints that help the patient recover more quickly than she would otherwise. ATs teach patients how to change their environment to keep them from being reinjured and how to perform exercises at home to aid in their recovery.

Professional Health and Well-Being

Athletic trainers are also trained to manage facilities that provide health care services to clients and patients. From complying with state and federal laws to protecting patient privacy through the Health Insurance Portability and Accountability Act (HIPAA), ATs can successfully run a clinic or a private practice using their skills and training. Like physicians, ATs can have their services paid for by health insurance, but they must maintain accurate patient records to keep track of when they treated a patient and the services they provided.

Athletic trainers are no longer limited to treating athletes on the fields and courts of high schools, colleges, and professional teams. They are also vital members of the health care team in hospitals, clinics, and doctors' offices throughout the country. In these medical settings, they provide care and education for patients who have had surgery or who have experienced an injury in a nonathletic setting.

ATs are becoming part of the health care team for jobs that require a large amount of physical strength and endurance as well. Police and fire departments, and the military, are hiring ATs to keep their personnel healthy and well.

ATs are also able to provide treatment and assistance right in the workplace so patients don't have to miss valuable work time to travel to and from a doctor's office. Manufacturing and construction businesses are hiring ATs to create safer work-spaces and treat acute injuries on site, saving the businesses tens of thousands of dollars in lost work time and medical costs. The scope of an AT's practice is expanding, creating more opportunities nationwide for those wanting to help people simply feel better.

 Text-Dependent Questions

1. What is an allied health care professional and what role do allied health care professionals play in contemporary health care?
2. What are the five roles of an athletic trainer?
3. Why is injury prevention such a key element in the work of athletic trainers?

 Research Project

The next time you are at a sporting event, observe the kinds of things the athletic trainers are doing for their athletes. Make notes about what you see and look up why those things help athletes, even if they are not injured.

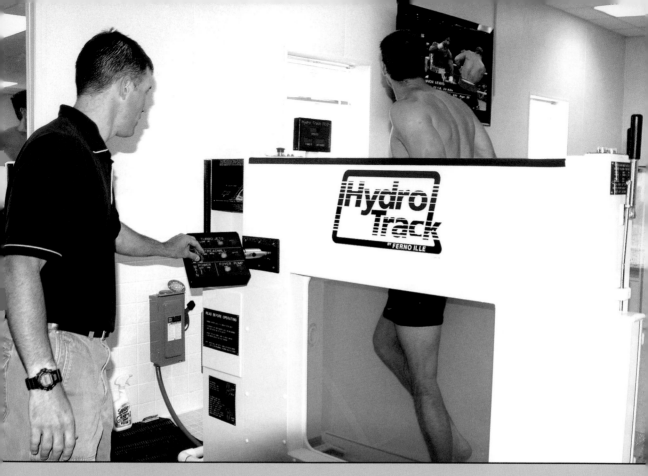

An athletic trainer adjusts the underwater treadmill for a patient.

 Words to Understand in This Chapter

concussion—a traumatic brain injury that alters the way the brain functions.

occupational settings—places where people work.

orthopedics—the branch of medicine that focuses on bone and muscle.

rehabilitate—to restore someone to health or normal life by training or therapy after an injury or an illness.

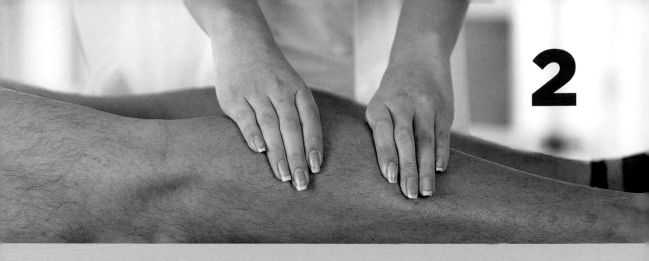

2

A Look at the Opportunities

Athletic trainers have been recognized by the American Medical Association as part of the allied health care team for nearly 30 years. According to the U.S. Department of Labor's Bureau of Labor Statistics, the job prospects for athletic trainers are expected to grow by 21 percent in the next decade, much faster than the average growth rate of other professions. This is largely because athletic trainers are able to fill a need for injury prevention and treatment, not just in sports, but in schools and businesses as well.

While high school and college students who assist in athletic training duties are called "athletic training student aides" or "student athletic trainers," athletic trainers (ATs) hold a bachelor's or a master's degree from a school that is accredited by the Commission on Accreditation of Athletic Training

Education (CAATE) and have certification from the Board of Certification (BOC) of the athletic trainer. In every case, athletic trainers collaborate with physicians to help patients perform their best in athletics as well as the activities of work and daily life.

In order of pay and demand, some of the most popular job settings for athletic trainers are in the following areas.

Colleges and Universities

One of the largest groups employing athletic trainers are colleges and universities. Every division of the National Collegiate Athletic Association (NCAA) employs ATs to help prevent and treat injuries, not only of athletes who compete on varsity teams at the intercollegiate level, but also those who play intramural or club sports on campus. The median salary for ATs in all areas of education is about $47,540.

ATs work to *rehabilitate* more than 460,000 student athletes at over 1,000 colleges across the country. In a report released by the NCAA, more than half of injuries sustained by those student athletes were to the lower extremities, including the feet, legs, knees, and hips. While contact sports, such as football and wrestling, tend to have the highest injury rates, sports that limit or prohibit contact, such as soccer and basketball, still have significant

Educational Video

Take a look inside a football locker room.

Professional sports teams employ athletic trainers to attend to their athletes. Here, a trainer with the Houston Astros checks a player who has been hit by a pitch.

numbers of injuries that are caused by contact between players. As a result, athletic trainers in colleges and universities develop prevention strategies that focus on balance, coordination, and strength to keep athletes on the field or on the court.

Secondary Schools

In an ideal scenario, a team physician would be present at every high school game and practice to ensure the safety of the students. Unfortunately, due to budget and time constraints, this is not possible. In many cases, coaches or parent volunteers with basic first aid training are left to attend to injured athletes. With emerging research about the long-term effects of repeated *concussions* in the developing brain, many high schools have turned to athletic trainers to provide immediate care for injuries, like concussions, as well as working with coaches to prevent these kinds of injuries from happening in the first place.

Athletes are less likely to aggravate existing injuries when the directions of an athletic trainer are followed. What's more, full-time secondary school athletic trainers are available during the day to help injured athletes implement recovery instructions from their team or personal physician. Such services speed healing time and reduce the amount of time students lose in the classroom.

Hospitals and Clinics

Athletic trainers are regularly employed in hospitals and clinics to improve patient care. The median wage for ATs in such settings was $45,270, according to the most recent data. ATs who are part of *orthopedic* and sports medicine practices take a patient's history, perform an evaluation, provide instruction on exercises the patient can do at home, and educate patients on how to keep from reinjuring themselves in the future. These ATs may also be used in family and pediatric practices to help patients with physical disabilities strengthen their bodies so they can perform daily tasks.

It is becoming increasingly common for ATs to work with

A group of people work on their recovery using exercise machines.

physicians and physical therapists in other clinical settings, too. Skilled nursing facilities, also known as nursing homes, often employ ATs and physical therapists together. Working in tandem, these professionals help the elderly and severely disabled regain strength and mobility. ATs may also conduct group exercise classes designed to enable residents to regain and maintain balance and coordination.

To work with physicians in a hospital or clinic, ATs don't need additional training or certification beyond a bachelor's degree and certification by the Board of Certification (BOC). They do need to have a desire to interact with people of all ages and physical abilities, since the majority of their patients will not be traditional athletes.

Occupational and Military Settings

An emerging area of practice for athletic trainers is in *occupational settings*—especially manufacturing and industrial workplaces—and the military. The physical demands placed on people who work in construction and manufacturing often result

The military uses athletic trainers to keep their service members in the best shape possible.

in injury. If we think of them as "industrial athletes," it is easy to see why they would have a need for ATs. Many industrial employees carry large, heavy loads from one location to another, are strapped into harnesses hundreds of feet aboveground, or have to work with their arms overhead for eight hours a day. ATs can help them reduce the likelihood of injury by providing them with occupational safety equipment or methods for strengthening their bodies.

The military has begun using ATs to create programs to reduce injuries to soldiers, both in training and in the field. During basic training, ATs design programs that reduce the likelihood of injury to those who may not have experienced rigorous physical training before. In the field, ATs set up medical treatment units where soldiers who are injured can be immediately evaluated and sent to the appropriate care team for further treatment.

ATs have begun to appear everywhere, from NASA to police departments, giving employees the ability to be evaluated and treated without having to leave their job. The median salary for athletic trainers in occupational and military settings is $43,070, according to the most recent data available. These are also among the fastest-growing areas for athletic trainer jobs.

Professional Athletics and Performing Arts

While professional athletics and performing arts are the most flashy areas of athletic training, they are by no means the most common. Only accounting for 5 percent of all athletic trainers

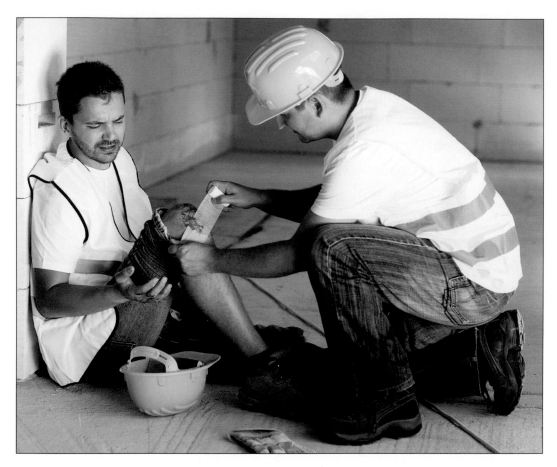

Industrial businesses are using athletic trainers to treat employees and limit the amount of work time a person loses after an injury.

in the industry, ATs in this realm can expect to earn a median salary of $44,920, often with travel required. Like those in colleges and universities, ATs in professional athletics and performing arts use their knowledge of the human body to examine footwear, technique, equipment, and an athlete's physiology for ways to prevent injury. Then, they can help team or company physicians attend to athletes or performers who become injured. As a bonus, ATs who work in professional athletics and the performing arts often get the best seats in the house. While this area of the profession is extremely competitive, it does not require additional training or skills beyond an athletic trainer's initial education and certification.

Text-Dependent Questions

1. What does the acronym BOC stand for?
2. What do athletic trainers do in hospitals and clinics?
3. What is the fastest-growing sector for athletic trainers?

Research Project

Talk to an athletic trainer in one of the areas that interests you the most. Ask him how he got his job, what he likes about it, and what he wishes he could change. If possible, follow him on the job for a few hours to see firsthand what being an athletic trainer in that environment is like.

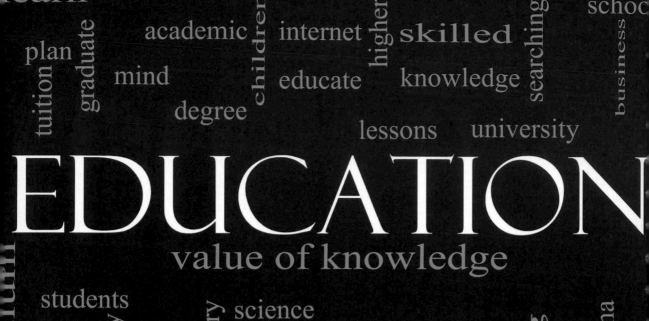

In order to become an athletic trainer, a person must complete a Bachelor's or Master's degree in Athletic Training and pass a licensing exam.

 Words to Understand in This Chapter

accredited—referring to a college or university program that has met all the requirements established by a particular national organization for a specific job (accreditation amounts to the official stamp of approval for a degree).

continuing education—classes that are designed for professionals to improve their skills and stay up-to-date on the latest practices in their field.

diagnosis—the determination of what is wrong with a patient; this process is especially important because it will guide the type of treatment the patient receives.

dissertation—a lengthy research paper about what a doctoral candidate finds out in conducting his or her research.

reconditioning—the process of helping patients become as strong as they were before their injuries.

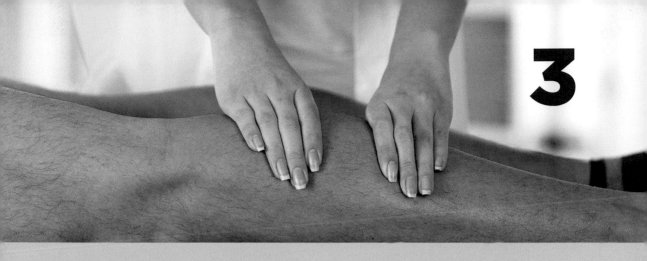

Education and Training

Becoming a certified athletic trainer is not as easy as it sounds. First, you must receive a bachelor of science or a master of science degree from one of 450 *accredited* college or university programs. Once you have completed your degree, you must then take and pass the Board of Certification (BOC) exam. Only then can you receive certification and call yourself an athletic trainer. Even after you receive licensing as a certified athletic trainer, you must then complete *continuing education* classes in order to stay up-to-date on the latest techniques for diagnosing and treating patients. While the process may seem overwhelming, it is manageable when broken down into parts.

The process of becoming an athletic trainer involves both classroom instruction and clinical practice.

Bachelor of Science Degree

First, it is important to select a university or college that meets your needs. Begin with the list of accredited colleges and universities and narrow it down by location, university size, and how competitive the program is. Other things to consider are tuition and fees, distance from home or family, the number of people admitted to the program each year, and the extracurricular activities the college or university offers. Be sure to ask about graduates' pass rate on the BOE exam. If a school does not have a high pass rate, look elsewhere. This means the school's curriculum is not as effective in preparing students for the BOE exam as it should be. After you choose a college or university— or several of them—where you'd like to study, you will apply for admission.

Educational Video

Listen to an athletic trainer talk about her job.

Once you are accepted as a student at the university, you will meet with an academic adviser who can outline the classes you need to take to earn your degree. These classes will include study in basic sciences, such as human anatomy and physiology, chemistry, biology, statistics, and kinesiology. Once you have successfully completed these classes, you will take courses in six areas of the athletic training practice—injury prevention, *diagnosis*, emergency care, treatment, *reconditioning*, and administration.

Clinical Practice

To earn accreditation, colleges and universities agree to teach students in the classroom, and to give them a chance to put into practice all the things they have learned. These opportunities, called clinical practice, are a way for students to practice diagnosing and treating real patients under the supervision of certified athletic trainers. Colleges and universities often do this by letting student athletic trainers diagnose and treat athletes who attend the same school. This may be done during a game or a match, or afterward in a university training facility.

Another way students receive clinical practice is by arrangement with local hospitals and clinics where athletic trainers are currently working. This helps student trainers gain a wide variety of experience. Clinical practice makes up two years of a student's studies and prepares student athletic trainers for the BOC exam.

Master of Science Degree

In some cases, people who already have a bachelor of science degree in a field other than athletic training want to become athletic trainers. These people may apply for admission to a master of science degree program in athletic training. These programs are designed much like bachelor of science programs, so that a person will be able to pass the BOC exam at the end of their studies. Students must complete the same basic science courses in human anatomy and physiology, biology, chemistry, statistics, and kinesiology and advanced courses in diagnosing, treating, and rehabilitating people with injuries. Students must also complete similar clinical experiences to the bachelor of science degree. The main difference between the bachelor's and master's degree programs is the introduction of research into the field of athletic training. Candidates for master of science degrees must complete a research project or paper that is aimed at improving the way athletic trainers diagnose or treat patients.

According to the National Athletic Trainers' Association, in the near future those who wish to become athletic trainers will only be able to do so once they receive master's degrees. However, people who have already completed their bachelor's

Students learn about anatomy and physiology, biology, chemistry, and kinesiology.

degrees and obtained their certifications will be accepted as athletic trainers and will not be required to earn a master's degree in order to continue working. Still, the movement toward graduate education will eventually leave those without a master's degree unable to compete with those who do have this credential.

Board of Certification (BOC) Exam

The Board of Certification (BOC) has been responsible for certifying athletic trainers since 1969. Once a person has graduat-

In addition to classroom instruction, athletic training students must complete clinical rotations to practice what they have learned.

ed with a bachelor's or a master's degree in athletic training, he can sit for the BOC exam. A student who is in his last semester of school can also take the BOC exam in order to make sure he is certified and ready for a job when he graduates. Anyone with a degree in athletic training has up to two years to pass the BOC exam.

A candidate applies for approval to take the BOC exam. This approval is signed by someone at her college or university showing that she has completed the education requirement.

The candidate can then schedule and pay for her exam. On the day of the exam, she will take an Internet-based test resulting in a score between 200 and 800. A score of 500 is considered a passing grade and certification can be awarded two to four weeks after the test.

Continuing Education

Even after you achieve certification as an athletic trainer, you will still be required to keep learning. Continuing education is important to an athletic trainer in maintaining not only his skills but his certification as well. Certified ATs are required to complete 25 continuing education units (CEUs) per year through programs that have been preapproved by the BOC. To earn CEUs, certified ATs may complete home-based coursework; attend workshops, seminars, or conferences; take postcertification classes offered by colleges and universities; or write academic papers for publication. These CEUs help ATs stay on the cutting edge of their industry and explore new knowledge in areas where they may not have experience. They also give ATs a chance to master new techniques and therapies to better help their patients recover from injury or surgery.

Doctoral Degree

Some athletic trainers want to enter the world of higher education, so they can train future athletic trainers. Very few universities offer a doctorate in athletic training, and admission to these programs is highly competitive. However, once you complete a doctorate, you are ready to teach students at colleges and universities who want to be athletic trainers. Those with

Once you have completed your degree, you must pass the Board of Certification exam.

doctoral degrees also play a vital role in conducting research that changes the way all athletic trainers diagnose and treat patients.

In order to receive a doctoral degree, students must apply to the program and become doctoral candidates. These candidates may be required to take some classes, but the majority of their time is focused on teaching other athletic training students and researching new methods for performing AT duties. Once they have completed their research and written a *dissertation*, doctoral candidates must present what they have learned to a board who will determine if they have met the requirements for a doctorate degree. They are then called by the title "doctor" and are ready to begin a career at a college or university.

Like those in many health care professions, athletic trainers take a lot of science classes over the course of their education. These are very difficult classes, often with extra lab work and a lot of memorization. If you want to become an athletic trainer, the best preparation for this career is to sign up for science classes in high school. By studying biology and chemistry in high school, you are becoming familiar with the content of the classes you will be taking in college. Advanced placement and concurrent enrollment science classes have the added benefit of giving you college credit while you're still in high school.

 Text-Dependent Questions

1. What is the main difference between a bachelor of science degree in athletic training and a master of science degree in athletic training?
2. Why is continuing education important for athletic trainers?
3. What does a doctorate prepare you to do?

 Research Project

Find a college or university near you that offers a bachelor's or master's degree in athletic training and is accredited through the Commission on Accreditation of Athletic Training Education. (Visit http://caate.net/search-for-accredited-program/ to find one near you.) Make an appointment with an academic adviser to talk about the kinds of classes you can take now to prepare you for admission to their college or university program.

Athletic trainers also help athletes prevent injury by correctly performing exercises.

 Words to Understand in This Chapter

biomechanics—the study of the mechanical laws relating to the movement or structure of living organisms.

poultice—a soft mass of plant material that is applied to the skin to relieve soreness and inflammation.

standardize—to help create and maintain a uniform level of quality.

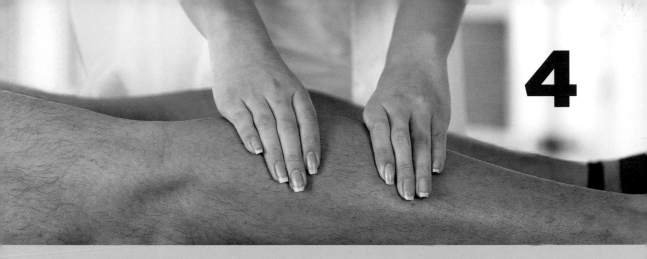

The Evolution of Athletic Training

There are currently more than 45,000 certified athletic trainers in the United States who work with physicians to prevent, diagnose, and rehabilitate injuries in athletes, people with disabilities, or those who have had surgery. While athletic training is currently considered part of the health care team, the profession has humble beginnings.

Athletic Training Begins

Athletic training in the United States dates back to 1881, when a man named James Robinson was hired by Harvard University to help the football team get into better shape. At the time, the term athletic trainer meant someone who worked with track and field athletes, but Robinson was one of the first

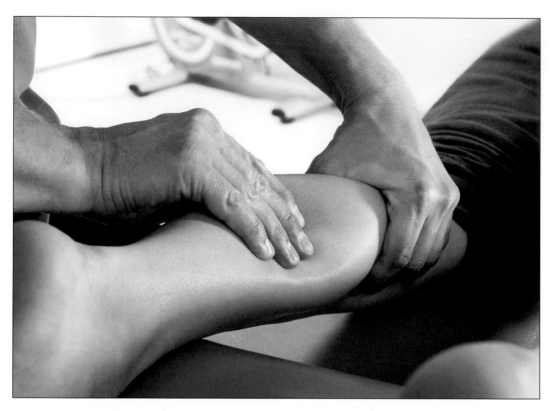

An athletic trainer uses massage to relieve pain in a calf injury.

to apply the same principles to other sports. His primary focus was to help athletes prevent injury altogether, but he also worked with them once they were injured.

The first major textbook on athletic training was published in 1917. Written by Samuel E. Bilik and titled *The Trainer's Bible*, this book had no little technical information about the human body and its functions. Instead, it instructed athletic trainers to apply rubs or *poultices* to different parts of the body and prescribe home exercises to speed recovery. While many principles presented in *The Trainer's Bible* have been superseded by tenets of modern science and technology, the profession would not be what it is today without the foundational ideas of its author.

NATA Is Organized

The National Athletic Trainers' Association (NATA) was established in 1950 in an effort to *standardize* both the duties of an athletic trainer and the curriculum that was used to train ATs to do their job. The first curriculum was developed by NATA in 1959 and adopted by several universities. It focused not only on how to perform the duties of an AT, but also on how to teach health and physical education. This was intentional, since most ATs were working in schools that would not hire them to perform athletic training duties full time. So, in order to keep a full-time job, ATs were required to teach physical education (PE) as well. Classes in this first curriculum included human anatomy, biology, and chemistry, as well as courses on classroom management and education techniques.

Even though the curriculum was developed in the late 1950s, it was not until 1969 that the first undergraduate athletic training programs were officially recognized by NATA. After a person completed his degree, he was required to intern with an athletic trainer in order to practice the techniques he had used in class. During this time NATA began to develop a national certi-

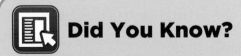

Did You Know?

The National Athletic Trainers' Association (NATA) was founded in 1950 when 200 athletic trainers gathered in Kansas City, Missouri to talk about ways to improve the field. Today the organization has more than 40,000 members.

fication exam to ensure that all athletic trainers across the country had a similar knowledge and skill base.

Athletic Training Becomes an Allied Health Care Profession

During the 1970s and 1980s, ATs were taking on more of a health care role and less of an education role. In response, NATA began to restructure its curriculum requirements to eliminate classes focusing on how to teach health and physical education. Replacing them were courses on exercise, diagnosing and preventing injuries, and *biomechanics.* It was not until June 1990 that the American Medical Association (AMA) formally recognized athletic training as an allied health care profession, similar to nursing and physical therapy. NATA then transferred the job of accrediting schools to an organization that would eventually become the Committee for Accreditation of Athletic Training Education (CAATE).

Oftentimes, the job of an AT is still confused with that of a personal trainer. While an AT may perform some of the tasks a personal trainer does, an AT's knowledge, skills, training, and experience are much more extensive than that of a personal trainer, qualifying an athletic trainer as an allied health care professional.

Introducing Clinical Education

As the classroom curriculum for athletic trainers shifted away from education and toward health care, these new athletic trainers needed opportunities to practice what they were learning. In 1994, a total of 18 initiatives were developed by an educational task force to do away with the internship requirement in favor of clinical training and education while students were still in school. Instead of simply learning about athletic training in the classroom, graduating, and being expected to perform the duties of an athletic trainer, students were given opportunities to work beside certified athletic trainers while they were still in school. These controlled situations let the students see firsthand how to perform some of the techniques they were learning in class, and try their hand at performing them as well.

In 2001, clinical requirements were expanded to encompass not only sports medicine, but also physical therapy clinics, rehabilitation clinics, emergency rooms, physicians' offices, and college

Athletic trainers are becoming more common in industrial, manufacturing, and construction businesses. Here, they focus on accident and injury prevention by teaching employees how to lift, stretch, carry, and climb.

and university health centers. Student athletic trainers are exposed to upper extremity injuries (arms, neck, hands, fin-

Educational Video

Scan here for an overview of the history of athletic training.

gers), lower extremity injuries (legs, knees, ankles, feet), and injuries involving multiple parts of the body in both men and women. Not only did this help students become more well-rounded professionals, it also helped them discover the environment in which they wanted to work.

Athletic Training Today

The majority of certified athletic trainers today join NATA to support their profession and network with other athletic trainers. NATA strives to offer resources and services that help ATs enhance their skills and stay up-to-date on the latest trends and techniques in athletic training. The organization also offers continuing education classes to help certified athletic trainers maintain their certification.

According to the U.S. Department of Labor's Bureau of Labor Statistics, athletic trainers today make an average yearly salary of $46,940. The highest-paid athletic trainers work for businesses to prevent injuries in industrial and manufacturing settings. These ATs earn an average of $69,700 a year. While ATs are relatively new to this sector, they offer an important service. As ATs work to prevent on-the-job injuries, workers in turn reap the benefit of less downtime, no loss of pay, and an ability to have more productive years in their career. However, should a worker become injured on the job, ATs can often save businesses money by treating injuries on site, rather than sending employees to third-party clinics.

The majority of athletic trainers work in hospitals, clinics, physicians' offices, or other medical settings. With increasing health care costs, these areas are looking for ways to improve physician productivity without sacrificing patient satisfaction. That is where ATs come in. They teach patients how to perform therapy and strengthening exercises on their own. They take patient histories and perform diagnostic tests. They free up a physician's time to see more patients and treat more complex cases with the time and care that is needed. An AT in a

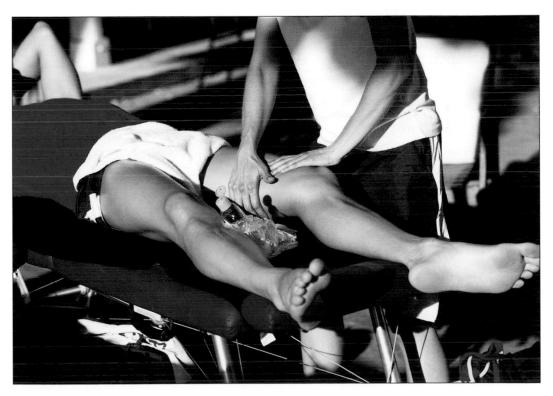

Events like marathons, obstacle races, or triathlons often have athletic trainers on hand to attend to athletes should injuries occur.

Once an athlete is on the road to recovery, an athletic trainer's job is to make sure they do not become injured again.

hospital, clinic, or physician's office makes an average of $46,600 a year.

The next largest group of ATs in the workforce ply their trade in the educational setting. These athletic trainers work to prevent injuries to student athletes while treating any injuries that may occur. ATs are able to treat emergency situations through their knowledge of first aid and CPR. They also work with physicians to help students recover from injury without missing important classroom time.

The highest average annual salary for ATs is found in the Houston, Texas area and averages $66,850. Texas also leads the country with the total number of AT jobs, while Connecticut has the largest concentration of ATs in the country.

 Text-Dependent Questions

1. Where did the first athletic trainer work in the United States?
2. When did the American Medical Association officially recognize athletic training as an allied health care profession?
3. Where do the highest-paid ATs generally work?

 Research Project

Talk to an athletic trainer who has been working for more than ten years. Ask her how the profession has changed over the course of her career. Ask her what advice she would give someone who was interested in becoming an athletic trainer.

Skilled athletic trainers are in demand in many industries and professions, not just sports.

 Words to Understand in This Chapter

agility—the ability to be quick and graceful.

modalities—a symptom or pattern that aids in diagnosis of an injury or illness.

ultrasound—medical imaging that uses sound frequencies to create a visual picture of an injury.

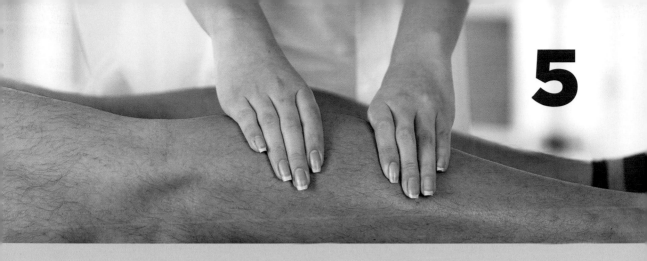

Overview and Interview

Certified athletic trainers are often the first responders when an athlete is injured. Like the EMTs of the field or the court, they quickly assess the severity of an injury and decide on a course of action to prevent further injury. With an expected 21 percent increase in job growth over the next decade, athletic trainers are no longer consigned to the field of play, but are being welcomed as members of the health care team in every setting. Still primarily responsible for helping doctors diagnose and treat injuries in student and professional athletes alike, ATs can apply their expertise to every person who moves. Athletic trainers are helping postsurgical patients regain their strength and mobility in hospitals and

clinics. They are working in factories and manufacturing plants to prevent and treat workplace injuries. In addition, they are popping up on military bases around the world to keep service members physically strong and active after injuries.

Educational Video

Scan here for a look at a day in the life of a University of Texas athletic trainer.

Q&A with a Professional in the Field

Shaleese White

What follows is a transcript from an interview with Shalecse White, a certified athletic trainer working in the field today.

QUESTION: How long have you been an athletic trainer?

Shaleese: "Seven months."

QUESTION: What inspired you to get into this field?

Shaleese: "I always knew I wanted to be in the medical field. In second grade I wanted to be a pediatrician, but I started playing sports and injuries happened. That was when I discovered that there was a person who could help fix injuries. It combined my love of athletics and my love of medicine in one field."

QUESTION: Tell me a little about the schooling/training you need to become an athletic trainer. How many years did you attend college? What types of classes did you take? What kind of hands-on training were you required to complete in order to obtain your degree?

Shaleese: "It took me a total of four years to complete my bachelor's degree in athletic training. I had an advantage because I knew right away what I wanted to do. That gave me a chance to take the prerequisite courses for admission into the program as my general education courses. I took classes like anatomy and physiology, biology, and statistics in my first few years of school. I also took basic first responder courses and became CPR-certified, which is a requirement for admission into the program as well.

"Once I was a student in the athletic training program, I took classes in exercise physiology, *modalities*, rehabilita-

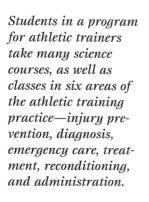

Students in a program for athletic trainers take many science courses, as well as classes in six areas of the athletic training practice—injury prevention, diagnosis, emergency care, treatment, reconditioning, and administration.

tion, and taping. We were fortunate enough to have a class on spinal dysfunction, which is something not many programs offer. A lot of times you are taught that if there is an injury to the spine, you have to refer the person to a specialist. We were actually taught how to diagnose and rehab less severe spinal injuries.

"Our program didn't hold all of the clinical work until just before graduation. Instead, all our coursework was supplemented with a clinical rotation as soon as we were finished with the classroom instruction. So rather than learning about everything in athletic training, then trying to remember in clinicals what you learned two years before, we had a chance to practice the things we were learning as soon as we learned them.

"We were also required to have 5 hours of observation, 1,200 clinical hours, and 20 additional general medical hours where we interned with a physician. I had the chance to work with the on-campus physician's office and the club sports physician."

QUESTION: How did you get your current job with a professional sports team?

Shaleese: "It actually started with an internship through my university. I was able to move into a paid position once that internship was over. I am currently in graduate school in the off-season working on my master's in health sciences with an emphasis in athletic training."

QUESTION: Is this job what you expected when you first made the decision to get into this field?

Shaleese: "From the beginning I wanted to work with a professional team. As an athletic trainer for a high school, you work with several sports at a time. Not only do you have to know the types of injuries that are common to every sport, it is almost impossible to be at every sporting event, every time. When working with a college or professional team, you can focus on one sport at a time."

QUESTION: What kind of technology do you use each day?

Shaleese: "We don't use a lot of technology to diagnose injuries. We will send someone for an x-ray on occasion, but most of the time we use our hands to diagnose a problem. We also use electrical stimulation, laser, and *ultrasound* therapies as well as a host of other devices to measure balance, strength, and *agility*. Most of our documentation is done on computers, tablets, or smartphones, so we can keep track of where everyone is in their progress."

QUESTION: What surprised you the most once you were out of school and in the field?

Shaleese: "I was shocked to find out how many people have no clue what athletic trainers do. When most people hear that I am a certified athletic trainer, they will mistake me

Athletic trainer Shaleese White shows off a few of the tools she uses on a daily basis.

for a personal trainer. Then when they find out that I work in the sports field, they assume all I do is tape ankles. While I can certainly help athletes become stronger and faster, and I can certainly tape an ankle, there is more to it than that. Most people don't understand that we are part of the medical field."

QUESTION: What has been the most challenging aspect of your job?

Shaleese: "There are two things. First, being a woman in the field is sometimes difficult. There are a lot of female athletic trainers out there, but very few who work with men's professional teams. You have to learn how to stand your ground because players want to play. Coaches want them to play. But you have to do what's in the best interest of the athlete.

"The second is helping athletes understand injuries that they don't see, especially in the case of concussions. Again, it goes back to doing what's best for the athlete, regardless of what they think you should do."

QUESTION: What is the most rewarding aspect of the job?

Shaleese: "I have the best seat in the house to every game! In all seriousness, when you run out onto the field and you make eye contact with an athlete who is injured, they always have a look of relief like, 'Okay. Help is here.'" That's the moment when you know you're making a difference.

QUESTION: What would you say to a young adult considering athletic training as a career?

Shaleese: "Don't let one or two bad experiences discourage you from continuing your education and getting certified. You will have days when you think to yourself, 'I have no idea what I'm doing.'" Those happen to everyone. The trick is to just keep going, keep learning, and keep trying.

QUESTION: What kind of personal traits do you think are important for an athletic trainer?

Shaleese: "The ability to improvise, adapt, and overcome. That has become my personal mantra and it's all-encompassing. You will have crazy things happen that were never in the textbook. You will be forced to improvise a strategy based on what you do know. There is a constant stream of new information and new techniques and you can't get stuck in your ways. You have to adapt your strategies as you go. Then, you have to overcome your need to please other people. There will come a time when a coach needs a player who isn't ready and you have to stand by your decision to keep them on the bench. It's hard, but you have to do what's in the long-term best interest of the player."

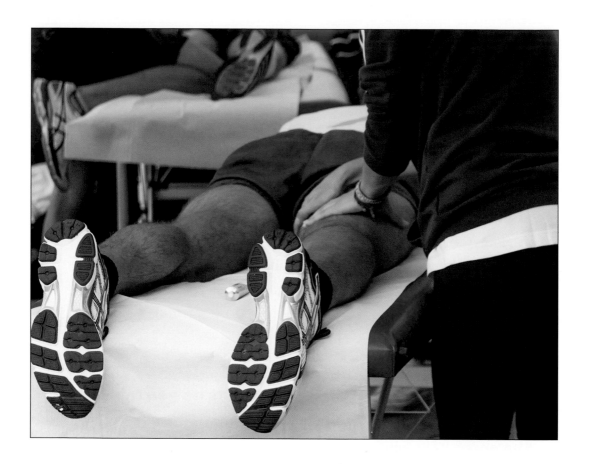

QUESTION: Working for a professional sports team requires different hours than a normal corporate job. What sort of toll does it take on you physically and socially to work such odd hours?

Shaleese: "When you're on season, you miss family gatherings and chances to be with your friends, but the people you work with become your friends. Most people don't understand that we're the first people at the stadium and the last people to leave. We're often there two to three hours before game time and two to three hours after. Then there are six-hour training days in between games when we are working with athletes who are injured as well as athletes who are trying to improve their performance. You sacrifice time with your loved ones sometimes, but I love what I do."

QUESTION: In your mind, what makes for a successful athletic trainer?

Shaleese: "You have to be passionate about your job, no matter how long you do it. You cannot lose sight of the fact that you're helping people. And you have to have a tremendous amount of integrity to be successful."

 Text-Dependent Questions

1. What kinds of ethical dilemmas does an athletic trainer with a professional sports team face?
2. What three characteristics do you need as an athletic trainer?
3. What is unusual about the schedule of an athletic trainer who works with a professional sports team?

 Research Project

Go to the Bureau of Labor Statistics website. Look up the salary and trends for athletic trainers in your state.

🔑 Series Glossary

accredited—a college or university program that has met all of the requirements put forth by the national organization for that job. The official stamp of approval for a degree.

Allied Health Professions—a group of professionals who use scientific principles to evaluate, diagnose and treat a variety of diseases. They also promote overall wellness and disease prevention in support of a variety of health care settings. (These may include physical therapists, dental hygienists, athletic trainers, audiologists, etc.)

American Medical Association (AMA)—the AMA is a professional group of physicians that publishes research about different areas of medicine. The AMA also advocates for its members to define medical concepts, professions, and recommendations.

anatomy—the study of the structure of living things; a person and/or animal's body.

associate's degree—a degree that is awarded to a student who has completed two years of study at a junior college, college, or university.

bachelor's degree—a degree that is awarded to a student by a college or university, usually after four years of study.

biology—the life processes especially of an organism or group.

chemistry—a science that deals with the composition, structure, and properties of substances and with the transformations that they undergo.

cardiology—the study of the heart and its action and diseases.

cardiopulmonary resuscitation (CPR)—a procedure designed to restore normal breathing after cardiac arrest that includes the clearance of air passages to the lungs, mouth-to-mouth method of artificial respiration, and heart massage by the exertion of pressure on the chest.

Centers for Disease Control—the Centers for Disease Control and Prevention (CDC) is a federal agency that conducts and supports health promotion, prevention and preparedness activities in the United States with the goal of improving overall public health.

diagnosis—to determine what is wrong with a patient. This process is especially important because it will determine the type of treatment the patient receives.

diagnostic testing—any tests performed to help determine a medical diagnosis.

EKG machine—an electrocardiogram (EKG or ECG) is a test that checks for problems with the electrical activity of your heart. An EKG shows the heart's electrical activity as line tracings on paper. The spikes and dips in the tracings are called waves. The heart is a muscular pump made up of four chambers.

first responder—the initial personnel who rush to the scene of an accident or an emergency.

Health Insurance Portability and Accountability Act (HIPAA)—a federal law enacted in 1996 that protects continuity of health coverage when a person changes or loses a job, that limits health-plan exclusions for preexisting medical conditions, that requires that patient medical information be kept private and secure, that standardizes electronic transactions involving health information, and that permits tax deduction of health insurance premiums by the self-employed.

internship—the position of a student or trainee who works in an organization, sometimes without pay, in order to gain work experience or satisfy requirements for a qualification.

kinesiology—the study of the principles of mechanics and anatomy in relation to human movement.

Master of Science degree—a Master of Science is a master's degree in the field of science awarded by universities in many countries, or a person holding such a degree.

obesity—a condition characterized by the excessive accumulation and storage of fat in the body.

pediatrics—the branch of medicine dealing with children.

physiology—a branch of biology that deals with the functions and activities of life or of living matter (as organs, tissues, or cells) and of the physical and chemical phenomena involved.

Surgeon General—the operational head of the US Public Health Department and the leading spokesperson for matters of public health.

Further Reading

Afremow, Jim. *The Champion's Mind: How Great Athletes Think, Train, and Thrive*. New York: Rodale, 2013.

Grover, Tim S. *Relentless: From Good to Great to Unstoppable*. New York: Scribner, 2013.

Webber, Matt. *Dropping the Bucket and Sponge: A History of Early Athletic Training*. Prescott, AZ: Athletic Training History, 2013.

Internet Resources

www.caate.net
> Website of the Commission on Accreditation of Athletic Training Education.

www.bls.gov/ooh/healthcare/athletic-trainers.htm
> This government website provides information on salaries and job outlook for athletic trainers.

www.nata.org
> Website of the National Athletic Trainer's Association.

Index

Numbers in **bold italic** refer to captions.

About the Author

Jennifer Hunsaker grew up wanting to become a pediatric surgeon specializing in cleft palate repair. Instead, she earned a Bachelor's Degree in Communicative Disorders and a Master's Degree in Human Resource Management and went on to work as a consultant for small businesses. Unsatisfied by the business world, she returned to her first love as a writer of medically-related content geared toward children, students, and those who work with them. When she isn't writing, she is chasing her husband, four children, and Yorkie named Wookie through the mountains of Northern Utah.